RED EARTH

By the same author

Poetry
Woe to the Boy
By the Black Stream
Odour of Blood
Nights in the Bad Place
The Selected Padraic Fiacc
Missa Terribilis
Ruined Pages: Selected Poems

Editor
The Wearing of the Black

RED EARTH

~~PADRAIC FIACC~~

Padraic Fiacc

13. xi. 96

LAGAN PRESS
BELFAST
1996

Acknowledgements are due to the following in whose publications and publishers under the auspices of which some of these poems have appeared: *Poetry* (Chicago), *Dolmen Press, Goldsmith Press, Blackstaff Press, University of California* and *Lapwing Press.*

Published by
Lagan Press
PO Box 110 BT12 4AB, Belfast

The publishers wish to acknowledge the financial assistance of the Arts Council of Northern Ireland in the production of this book.

ISBN: 1 873687 90 7
Author: Fiacc, Padraic
Title: Red Earth
Format: Paperback (138 mm x 210 mm)
1996

Cover Image: *Flight* (1977) by Brian Ferran
Set in Palatino
Printed by Noel Murphy Printing, Belfast

in memory of my dear poet-friend and comrade
Norman Dugdale

The meaning of the name of Adam is Red Earth

'I needed pagan words to tell it
I cannot remember being further
back than this dark earth
seeded in me wild great lust
madness, idol-worship ...'

—Rimbaud

CONTENTS

I

Conor

HURRICANE DEIRDRE
a forewarning

My hands on your belly can tell
The child kick and wrench until

Better not born the blond eye
Blazed blind of man, the boy.

A devastating child squeals
In your womb woman from burning

In the blood sea bodes no
True good cry that

At great speed the king going
Strong and high the sea road

This gold albino will
Eat the spokes out of the wheel.

MOORED

'You made up our life together.
You made it all up.'—Nancy

Quivering at the seaside singing
Tendrils sounding a bell
Scenting sand and sea
With each drifting petal

In the northeast wind the white
Lilacs blew
Over the black back
-yard wall, fell
Away forever for you and me

Not that proud anymore
With ash on our coat
Flown down from the mountain
Into the night that

Thin on the morning shore
Light through leaves of the glen
On Deirdre and Naisi and
Our 'dreamed only' boat
Will leave Scotland forever and

'Never such light again'.

A DEIRDRE GOODBYE

The grass is growing through
Our rooted in skull bone boat.
Your stormy north east
Sea wind washes clear
'Never such light again'.

Leave me alone on this cliff
Between the earth and the sky
Filling my basket with
Eggs which cannot be.

The run of the roe we ran
Till out of breath be
-grudged us so by
Brute man, that
Put-to-death boy
Will not let the bee sleep:

The run of the child or donkey
In wind for wings.

THE HUNTED LOVERS

In mild as a warm sea
A winter's evening
Daymoons in a rainbow
A star through water
We wait the kick
Of morning light
On a lonely islet
To the green east
The wild gold garlic's
Violet white
Silvering
Our interrupted sleep.

DEIRDRE TO DEATH

Do not fit to the grave
As foot to the shoe
This broken boy.
Push room in the red clay back
For the person will be not
That long after him you
Grief in the guise of a grave digger!
Set your grain
Against the torn eye
Children took the day
Star from by the root
That through the heart grow
The milk shoot of the blue
Clover flower for
The black bee was
My lover an hour or two
By the slow sea.

STORM

Deirdre sings a mad song

Boy-man with sunlight in your hair
Man-boy, moon-blue-eyed, that fair

O child dear

I am just asking you to go away.

I am burning burning in the sea.
I am burning burning in the clay.

You eat a peck of dirt before you die
And fare from it they say

The bit of grit and straw and grain
Burns into the porcelain.

I am crazed with the moon's shadow
The moon's shadow of the sun's light

The day's shadow of the light of night

Night burning slowly
The sun fallen lowly

Amongst thieves of grass and hay.

Would there never were

One more day.

DEIRDRE BETWEEN TWO RAMS

Blame not her raggedy beauty
Hung on wind
A petal on thorn ...

She slew the boy a-swim with her
In white-gold water loving him

She slew the mother fighting
Not to be born ...

Deirdre is dead
Dead at this wedding
Never having wished to die.

Deirdre ...

No man tuned nor taught her
    Death
        She loved a boy.

CONOR'S BELL SONG
Goodbye to Nancy

For you, stone shifted to an
Horizon of light. Walls fell.

Roof-tops tore, the valley had
The gashed open wound of a bed.

The winter-bound mountain river
Widened suddenly sea all silver

That your flight inflicted a wound
        That your eyes
Could not close on your poor

'Murderer' ...
    Barbarian
At the brink of things becoming

Frozen finish cracks the scum

Top hailstones on the pale
Ill flower of your fragile

Texture in the gale, I hear
Your agitated ear-rings still.

II

Mac Cuhal

KING CORMAC WATCHED HIS FATHER WITHER

At the hand harp, I, the son, saw
The dead rot loud in his hollow, that
(Rooted through bone) the mute mind gnaw,
Cracks at carrion heart
Slants like a dolmen down
The foot of the hacked hard hide.

A long deep clutter of rock-torn roots
Holding him still—standing up
Headless in a ditch. Here the foul

Bloated bile waters rise
Higher than the mountain is
Ever making a mound for the man

In the worm
In the seed
In the blood

In the bone
In the wound
In the child

In the ground.

THE BLACK GIANT

Dermot sings

Doomed to tragedy, that is, death,
Being beautiful, and so
Hold no mirror to my breath
Frozen in the snow

Wag no fist above my eyes
Open at you, not seeing you,
Tell to all the world no lies
Of me for myth more true

That he can be more human than
Woman in non human stare
And more of a man than a man
A hugging bear

Being tracked in the frost
By the little bloodhounds near
Lost or found he still is lost
Found frozen here.

FIONN'S SPRING

Casual now
Sky is off

Guard.

Thickening beech
Shadows air with
A light is
A Summer snow.

The stark
Naked cuckoo
Usen't to be
This so

Straight forward
As the sea
-bright black

Bird is.

THE FIRST DAY OF SUMMER

Wakening to a steep
Cliff of an Autumn

Lug-arm long
Wound-widening
Winter-sea day

Under bed sheets of
Ice at all dark gale
Of the horizon put
Pale with your eyes

Will not stay shut

Wakening to a blue
Fog, washing
The dead, as sea
Stone

I count the nights
Left but sea-spray
Dashed on a reef
Of time-black bone

Dwelling on
The fading moon:
You: GONE

It is
The end of Spring.

LAMENT OF GRAINNE ON THE ARM OF FIONN
She sings into herself

Sea light of an Autumn morning
Summery with shafts of coming
Night downing from sea-pine storming

I sang body to body to Dermot
In a bed of white gold grain:
A boy in my arms ... locked, unlocked

A look on his mouth without warning

The thousand kisses of the fragile
Shower of the fiercely churning
Waterfall of the mountain pool

Just do not think that I cannot still
Conjure out of stone wall you.

FIONN'S OLD AGE MAY SONG

Sound of land in snipe
Laughter of chirping
On the boughless island
-drowning sky

Natural as a boy
Wild as three starlings
Singing as a day
-tired child in the days
Of the long in
-between nights
And I heal by
One lone bee

Of a Summer's first fling
Starts up into a new
Storm-haze, buzzes

Of all times, things,
Places made glad
By the boy I once was,
The girl I once had.

THE BEGINNING OF THE STORMS

Oisin sings

Fionn in Norway came on
A sparrowy black pea cock
Tame as a pet, bold as a boy's son
Swinging over the loch
A woodlark at Sowan

Provoking appetite by dance of the beak
Gold, upturned
The warble of the note
Subtle to no knowing ear
Reaching, for the size of the throat

The wide carrying-over fjord-horizon
A song without word
The bird was human but
Clever, Fionn said, alert to his summon
He swore it could hear and understand

Finding no thing in the world 'queer'
Going into the hero's hand
As into his own due
I tell you, Patrick
That is why there are blackbirds in Ireland

Here in Derry Cairn
Swarming over, shadowing
Storm-lit Loch Erne
Fionn brought the creatures here
Started the swarm.

WINTER ON HIS BRIDE TO BE SPRING A CHILD

Fionn sings

The hair a fair May Day
Eyes, sunlit pear leaves,
    Two moons over the tiny mouth
    The star-green eyes.

The mouth:
    A little valley to the south.

She tosses her child-hair over her eyes.
Leaves of the copper pear-tree gleam.

    Grainne, daughter of the House of Art

Is granted me
As the sky grants the ground.
The fall of the hawthorn flower
The seed-bearing gold bee
The brilliant red holly bird.

Two eyes are morning heather
Star-green at moon light ...

    The small mouth
Looks an eye away from

My beard
Is flying
In the raining ice.

GLOSS

for Mary 'Bee' Denvir

Nor truth nor good did they know
But beauty burning away,
They were the dark earth people of old
Restive in the clay.

Deirdre watched Naisi die
And great King Conor of himself said
'Did you ever see a bottomless bucket
In the muck discarded?'

And comradely Dermot was destroyed by Fionn
Because of the beauty of a girl.
Because of the beauty of a girl
The sky went raging on fire

And the sea was pushed out into rage.
They were the dark earth people of old
And Deirdre pitched herself into the sea
Turn the page ... Turn the page.

STILLSCAPES

(i)

Before sky dark in dank mould
A May-dusted cat
Agates its paw

Polishes a grey face gold
Under coral azalea
In the removes of
The back meadow's shadow

Far from stone-throwing children
The sky, the brilliant black
Fionn loves

(ii)

The way the blackbird cocks its head
Listening for the teeth of the worm
A far-back scar of a window
As if at the end of a tunnel

Looks small

In the deafening silence just
Up to before the midsummer storm

Silences even

The thieving cuckoo's mating call.

THE GHOST
Grainne sings

Out of bull resentment
Snores to the moon
At black nightfall

By my side a skull
Hunted Dermot down:

In the land the lack
Of what was whole,

Flight of the great.
Loss of the seed.
Dermot dead.

I wed this rich old man's
Poor bed who lay
With a young boy
In a gold ditch

Glad on a past day
Of straw and dung
With the sing of his tongue
Filled me.

Gone. Gone.

I lie with a small wizened up
Old oxen-eyed head.

I stare at a boy
Tall from here to the moon

The eyes: gold pennies,
The hair: honey brown ...

Every night at the foot of the bed
He is my own one.

III

Mac Erca

NIGHTMARE FOR TYRANTS

Bare the bone to hang
A dog-bitten rag over
The gouged-out eye-stare

Press the rib down on
The hole in the bone
In the blood

Mutilate, behead, dismember
Man the strange god, charge

Him head down
To a pool on stone
Run him through with iron, he

He the hero, he
The horror will
Stand up headless and
Fight on.

MAN THE MYTH

(i)

'In his prime at the height of his power'

Moon on the wind, dead on the move
Sea red with the moon
And ghosts of the blood chill the mind
And I share this not knowing with a wide mankind.
The low snickering laugh of Maeve of Connacht gone.
Cú Chulainn good as no one.
Niall stuck upright in this mighty mound.
Cormac doomed to rule or rue or rot from birth.
Mock me, all, this dreaming boy
That in the mud red snow I
Am able to smell the great dead.

Dung in the stable steaming from
The earth bed
Poet glorified and sung.

Here, if I am a King
What distinguishes me as a King
Where is my realm—for

Struggling with the raw boned face
Of the herd boy driving the cow
I know more this scooped out falling
From under you grave bed of a place
Than the name of the thing that I am
A 'King' (stays up the night with the sow
For fear she eats her own litter).

Only let me live and increase as the wild
Bees left seed in the abandoned hive begot
The flower from the grain—God—
As the heads of the children tower
Over the dead man, do not
Know the power they wield, nor rank, who scarce
Out-rank the bird-laid day-eyes of the field.

(ii)

Centuries later children's children call
The tallness high if rooted deep the fall

Arms long stretched out wide
Rings you kick and creep through—strong.

Blind in vain glory to that he
Was scundered of blinding things also and

Stretching the man to fit the story—give
His helmet and his heels—the wings!

(iii)

Bin men
Wear rings

Against the stint
Of things

In Ireland still have

The slow grave walk of kings.

SÍN AT THE GRAVE OF MAC ERCA

You are still living
(I still want to call you friend)
Will bitterly
Laugh at my pity
That I, the dead one here,
That death is no end,
Would, blind, want to see
More horizon
Behind the tombstone
Blind with shadow or
O why should
Wild night wind, our love-child
Kick me in the womb?

IV

Brian

WITHOUT HER

(i)

Hot for war as sweating stallions are
Brave and bright as a cock on a tree
I am tired of creeping under the sky

Head in hand on fallen knee, but wait
Heatlightning through only
Earthware man and make what

He owns by High King born
Or lift up by letter of the law
Or let fall back down, cannot take

The hangdog streak out of my jaw
That I am bitter because I am
Alone

(ii)

That vagrant sea be made full
Ivies are rooted in the eyes
Of sunlit man, the blind bull

To see through shrouded moon-rise
Up over the cloud back onto light
A dreaming child-head, mock-fight

Wind with the butt of a breadknife
Old dead wars won by what
Child-bearing woman still will be

The clay-pit cover for
The worm of time from the beak of death if
Earth quarrels yet like a lover?

MIDNIGHT ON THE CAUSEWAY

Green lightning quivers
Each stone without stir
Evening dawns in
Mild moon air

On volcanic glass sand
Of the low-lying water
Wandering between iron earth
And rusted nowhere
A strange standing up dead wind

Bodily alienates nightmaring mind
To moss-barked, coal-black trees
Honied by roots the comb
Ages buried to radiate these
Once all Icelandic dry:
Now so thieving seas.

GORMLEY'S LAMENT FOR EVE
after Clontarf

I saw a man beating
A horse with a boat-oar.
He said, 'Go away you
This is not your affair
I can do what I like with my own horse sure.

Such the fine chirp
From the grub to
A king's daughter
Queen to three kings
And a king of the north for a son.

O my paps are sore
This long time
Without sucking of rage.
Blood congeals
To icy drips of Winter rain.

Father, brother, husbands, son
Kings of men each one
Under a sky scarred with swans
(Great black eagles
That the crowns sat on)

Go you down this road ahead
Of winter dark for me
This cold, old, tired

First banished woman.

MARAUDERS

Thorn in the hoof
Maggot in corn
Raven on the roof
Bats in the house

Hedgehog in the nest
Fox in the barn

Crows in the thatch
Waiting us
As the thieves
Watch.

HAG

More days keep coming on.
I recall a bull of a man.
Did not beauty break his back?

Here a thigh, there an arm
The mock-play of the sun-brown
Frowning storm-brow
That wound its way to
'Thundering things crack'.

Eyes went back into the head.
Frowns fell down:

Rattling in a sackcloth now
(Better clad before the moth
Sunk its teeth into the stitch)

The moth thought the gold braid
Great to wallow in

Chewed away the name
(Which fame or shame?)

When we were body to body brought
To the earth bed and death-laid
Great to wallow in ...

The child alone suckled my breast
Gave me its cry hungering hard
They cut in two with the sword
By a war won by wind by
Blast, beast and demon

Yes, coupled with commoner and king

And yet cannot tell which
So much dog goes into the thing
So much whining bitch

For want of the dog
The way that I am still
Unwanted by man or God.

SUNKEN FOREST

Fir under the wave
Oak, pine

Yew over the grave
Booted down in

The black ravens of prey
Croak and crow

Washed away by
A blue-jewelled sea
A melted mountain snow
The red pear tree

The hazel beech bough
Bones of the giant
Man and god
Land and the crown
Plenty and want

Make the bog
The gone down under
The west wanderer
The old blood
The new born
The wild wet cloud

An ivory cairn
Piles up on
Brendan like

Born gone.

SÍN THE SHE-SEER

Hanging on the skin
Of a vein twisted in
Side out

Robbed less one
Feuding skull and brute

Banging only
Of drying wind
Rusting the shoot

Bile of the bone adrift
On a river of shuddering
Liver
All the love left

An autumn leaf toss
Scumming
A rotten dry
Chirp and weep
Of the burning crisp flower

Corroded by hunger for
Man, the god
Does not have the power
To thwart the grave

I lie awake and think
These thoughts at
The earliest morning hour

Is

All the magic that I have.

AN OLD WOMAN ROAMS THE BATTLEFIELD AFTER CLONTARF

I go not in quest of a dead child
Years have taken
To the tops of pine cones
Nor nest fallen.
I roam the shore with a stone in my womb.
Where did all the dead come from?
There is no more place to go.
Gale blast has blown open
Doors of the tomb.
All lit with dark sea
Flashing light
Over the grinning dead
Is home.

SAINT COLMAN'S SONG FOR FLIGHT

Run like rats from the plague in you
Before death it is no virtue to be dead.
The cranog in the water, anywhere at all sure.
It is no virtue and it is not nature
To wait to writhe into the ground.

Not one in the Bible could see these dead
Packed on top of the other like dung
Not the two Josephs of Egypt
But would not run.

And Christ's blessing follow
(Is it not a blessing to escape storm?)

Pray to old Joseph, not a witless man
Who had the brains not to want to die

But when his time came only and at home in bed,
The door shut on the world, that wolf outside
Munching the leper's head

IRON AGE BATTLE

Sparks from flint
Blown by blast
To the smoking
Force of the fist

Herding factions
Of garrisons in
Up against the wall ...

The dismounting horsemen

That when the walls fall
Time's malice-hearted children
Clap their hands and laugh.
The mounts rear from the fire.

Afterwards
The old women stare
And shriek with the neighing
Deafened by the children's laughter

Cannot hear themselves dying.

SEED

By the Bath House where North Man
Thinned flesh by falling leaf
To the burn of the steaming wind
Seared petulant body brawn to bone

(Borne in the end by time, the thief
Far from Cahon's Tirkane)
Not a German Greek but out of mind
The slimy stone, the moss remain
And here and there in Maghera: the cinder

A small brickhaired boy whose ancestor
Was some orange Dane
Cannot yet say 'Da'
Answers back the centuries 'Yes Sir'

Strays near the Great Wall in witless disdain
Tramps barefoot on the skull of the charred emperor
Darts back up the blind back street
The Autumn coloured clouds his bedtime store

Himself the living trophy left
Of all that red gold gore.

TENTH CENTURY INVASION

Doves beat their wings
Against their breasts

Bloodying their wings
Bloodying their breasts ...

Bells ring throughout the book
At the bottom of the loch

Gold running over the
Ruined pages

Drowned
Emerald and lilac ink

From the song written in
The shaft of the sun

In the moment on the
Margin
Never to be sung.

V

Adam Street

ON ADAM STREET

for Jo Adamson

Knitting dust, bone by bone
With paper crackling tongue
Of rain at night on burning dung
I grope for the pagan word

Crows in the sea-crazed
Lidless with light eye of
The rock-snared tarn water's
Hag-ridden storm bird, but

No answers, just an
Almost flesh and blood-wrought ghost
Hundreds of human years, like lost
With wrong names on him of ancient kings

Dating the battle his hearsay number yet
His feeble fables messenger
More from the buried
If ingrowing roots

Than the text just printed by scholars
Most correct with each word caged
In mincing measure crude
Ship-wrecked sunken·treasure:

God-hungering man.

INNISFAIL LOST

Blond as sun on the tomb
An empty hearth ash-mould

Field-mice, running spiders bat
Shadow the earth-red throne ...

Regal lice dine and bloom
On bones blanketed in ermine

Furred with salt dust like seaweed ...

No magic, just time

Runs to seed on trophies once
Encased the Stone of Fate

Fall

All floor to down-flung door
Bare corrosion in ice-frozen rain

All sleeping here at night

Goats, pigs,

At their remove at dawn
Leave behind their dung ...

That is my song:

Man the ruin, king

Rory at the Monastery, Cong.

UNDER BLACK MOUNTAIN

'Tell me your trouble
I am your friend and brother'
—Lynch to Sweeny mad

Hunger hollows you out
And stretches beyond that even

Just do no
Ask me where I am going

Where rain starts on the sea
Where walls leaf-fly
To flower roots in bone

Where brief summer ends
Stripped man, body, tree,
Mind, soul, air, crack,

Crazy Sweeny of Ros
Earcain am I but for
The feather in me, bare

Flew all the way back
Down the mountain hill here.

Well then good
Crop in the ground.

THE KICKER

Tell thin layer of earth-capped skull
Red with the fire of clay in slime

Befriending the other in a ditch
Which the stranger which the brother

Hundreds of years later when
Office girls giggle with nerves at the look
Of the labouring man, himself took sick
By 'queer fumes', throws up on
All the land that the king owns and kicks
The bones out of the way of mounting bricks.

THE POET MYTH
'Initial Deception'

Taken in by the poet bit

That portrait painted by Nancy
after estrangement
                    how she
bone-netted light by charcoal from
   flesh gnawed off the skull
bone
for want of air, grey green as young

          skeleton soul ...

I sat so still, the spider on
my elbow made a clean get-a-way

Yet when she lined in a jaw (not mine)
                    of rock
to hint in time, when ripe enough

                    to stir

that sagging chin ought bone with
                    character
be broken
and obey the law and lock

I remembered
   not
being able to withhold howls of
bitter as the taste of toad
      blood

laughter
    for
the light was bitter and my eyes were dead.

Now
    tearing up some old love letter

I know
    the man she made
        I made

up out of
bits of
    torn into strips

writing paper ...

The poet is indebted to Dr. John Marshall for typing the original manuscript.